WISEBLOOD ESSAYS IN CONTEMPORARY CULTURE NO. 5

HOW TO THINK LIKE A POET

RYAN WILSON

WISEBLOOD BOOKS
2025

Copyright © 2019, 2025 Wiseblood Books & Ryan Wilson

Second Printing

WISEBOOD BOOKS
Joshua Hren, Editor-in-Chief
Post Office Box 870
Menonomee Falls, WI 53052
www.wisebloodbooks.com

ISBN: 978-1-951319-19-9

This book is for
Linda Defontes
and is dedicated to the memories of
David Ferry, Elise Partridge, Derek Walcott,
Richard Wilbur, and Franz Wright

HOW TO THINK LIKE A POET

Ἐὰν ταῖς γλώσσαις τῶν ἀνθρώπων λαλῶ καὶ τῶν ἀγγέλων, ἀγάπην δὲ μὴ ἔχω, γέγονα χαλκὸς ἠχῶν ἢ κύμβαλον ἀλαλάζον.

1 Cor. 13:1

All art is symbolic. If we understand a symbol to be the bodying forth of an abstraction, or the outward expression of the inward, all art is symbolic. Our culture, however, has difficulty in understanding this premise, and therefore has a limited ability to understand art of all varieties, especially, perhaps, literature. Our culture tends either to interpret literature in a purely literal way—as in reading a novel for the plot, or for the "relatable" quality of a character—or to concern itself purely with the ideas of a work—as in classrooms around the country where great books are taught as if they were mere receptacles for ideas, the primary concern being what students always call the "hidden meaning."

Now, of all readers, Catholic readers should not be susceptible to this dualism because the traditional Catholic reading of the Bible should, as Dante points out in his famous "Letter to Can Grande," teach us how to read. Yes, we are to read the Israelites' escape from Egypt as a literal, or historical, event, a factual event, but we are also to read that event as a figure for Christ's redeeming us from sin through salvation, as a figure for the Church Triumphant, and as a figure for each moment in our lives when we choose freedom in God's will over the slavery of our own will. That is, the Israelites' escape from Egypt is a symbol—it is a real and historical occurrence whose meaning is not limited by its historicity, whose meaning overflows that historical context, a visible sign of the invisible, if I may adapt a bit of the catechism. When we realize that all art worthy of the name strives for this symbolic quality, we will begin to read differently, to write differently, to see differently, and to think very differently.[1]

To get a better sense of how symbolism works in practice, we might consider briefly the Greek principle of ξενία (*xenia*), or "hospitality." Now, in the ancient world, xenia was of the utmost importance. The concern with hospitality permeates the works of antiquity, from Homer, through Aeschylus, Sophocles, and Euripides, and continuing through Vergil and Ovid. Indeed, this concern carries on into modern literature, and it is, *mutatis mutandis*, the concern of most contemporary theories about literature, which so often focus on "otherness." Therefore, xenia merits our consideration as a lasting and nearly universal concern.

Let's start with the *Odyssey*. Odysseus returns to Ithaka after twenty years away, but when he returns, he does so in disguise, as a peasant, and he tests the quality of xenia in Ithaka before proceeding to action. If we take this as mere plot, as merely literal events, we misunderstand Homer. Similarly, in Ovid's *Metamorphoses*, the old married couple, Baucis and Philemon, take in two strangers whom the rest of their townspeople have shunned. When the strangers turn out to be Zeus and Mercury, Baucis and Philemon are rewarded for their xenia by escaping the flood that destroys their town and by being transformed into two trees, an oak and a linden, that grow together as one, fulfilling the married couple's wish to be together forever. And again, we might consider the two strangers who appear to Lot in the city of Sodom, strangers whom the Sodomites want to rob. Lot, possessing xenia, is spared by these strangers, who turn out to be angels of the Lord, when the Lord decides to smite the entire city.

Do you see the pattern? Indeed, with this pattern in mind, we may profitably consider why Christ himself took on the form of an infant in a manger, rather than the form of an infant prince, why Christ himself wandered through desert places and entered into Jerusalem on a poor donkey. And we might question if this same pattern is not evident 1600 years later when Shakespeare writes *Measure for Measure*, in which the Duke disguises himself as a poor friar to test the xenia of the upstart politico, Angelo. Why are all these figures of power disguised as the poor and disenfranchised, as powerless strangers?

The reason is that the authors of these works, like Christ, are concerned with the health of the human soul, and the health of the human soul, whether that soul be pagan, Christian, or of any other faith, requires xenia, hospitality to the stranger. Moreover, whether these strangers are purely literary like Shakespeare's Duke, or possess historical reality, like Christ, their symbolic message is the more or less the same: it is our duty, and it is our salvation, or at least part of it, to demonstrate xenia, kindness toward strangers.

Now we often take this message in a purely literal manner. For instance, almost everyone knows the parable of the Good Samaritan from the Gospel of Luke, and almost everyone knows the parable means that we should be helpful to strangers in need, and that we should practice the theological virtue of *caritas*. But what if we take even Christ's parable of the Good Samaritan symbolically, as it was surely meant to be taken? It would then mean that we *not only* need to be kind to the literal and historical strangers we encounter, but that our souls *also* need to demonstrate xenia, or hospitality, to all that is unfamiliar, or strange. The implications of this xenia are far-reaching.

I'd like to focus briefly on the implications pertaining to knowledge and thought. What, in our symbolic understanding, constitutes the stranger? Would it not be all that is not familiar, all that is not already known and understood? Such seems to be the case. Our minds are, in a sense, hosts, and the world outside the mind is a stranger. Indeed, the world is always the stranger, always the man lying wounded on the roadside, beaten and robbed.

If we apply this concept of xenia to epistemology, we will be forced to consider not what we know, or how we know it, so much as how we approach knowledge. If the mind is a host, and the world is the stranger, our culture is generally composed of very poor hosts indeed. Our culture, rather than treating the stranger with hospitality, would enslave him, would force him to follow the comfortable customs of our household, would strip him of the dignity of difference and enlist him in menial tasks to make our home more comfortable and more profitable. We would make him speak our language, and do what we ask at every moment, bend down before our will and grovel at our feet.

We see all around us the dire consequences of such poor xenia. Our culture thinks of knowledge only as a means to power, a means to getting what we want: a grade, a job, a raise, a house, a car, fame, prestige, awards, and so on. Most of us treat the real world as a series of obstacles or impediments preventing the actualization of our personal idealized vision of what the world should be; most of us cannot even imagine what it would mean to treat the world with xenia. We dislike anything that is not exactly like us—though we shout "diversity" from the rooftops, really we're scandalized by difference; we attempt to bend nature, and other people, to our will; we learn about the world only to manipulate it and to control it for our own benefit, or to inflate our egos; we learn about others only to "network" or to use them more efficiently for our own ends. We turn the stranger into a slave, and whip him within an inch of his life, and, in so doing, we create chaos in the world around us; faction and violence appear; blood stains the streets of our cities; mountaintops and rainforests topple; the water seethes with pollution; civilization declines.

How, then, should we treat the stranger with xenia? What would that mean? It would mean to treat the world with respect, and with dignity, and with, above all, love.

Those whom we love we do not enslave. We value them for who they are, rejoicing to discover their similarities to us and thrilling to discover their differences from us. Our ambition, with those we love, is not always to get our way, or to win power, but our ambition is, quite simply, the pleasure of the beloved's company. This mutual love between host and stranger stands at the source of all happiness, for it liberates us from the grueling pursuit of desire, and the angry assertion of will, and the bitterness of the frustrated will, and it brings us nearer to God, who, we must remember, came to earth as a stranger, an outsider.

This type of xenia, when practiced spiritually, leads to spiritual health, and when practiced mentally, to mental health. To practice it is to love what we are not as what we are, to reconcile what is within us with what is without, to love our neighbors as ourselves, and to create harmony where our selfishness would create division. And we must not forget the great paradox underlying our xenia: the stranger, the guest, is always, in a deeper sense, the host. Odysseus was not truly a stranger but the king of Ithaka; Zeus and Mercury were not truly poor wanderers but gods; Shakespeare's Vincentio was not a poor friar but the Duke; Christ was not merely an itinerant wanderer but the Son of God, and the world may seem to us a guest for our minds to host, but we are, ultimately, the guests of the world, for it endures and we pass away. Similarly, what we know is not the host of reality; reality is the host, and our knowledge is the guest. Therefore, we should be circumspect in how we treat our guest, this stranger-world, for we are really *its* guests, as Mother Nature is forever inconveniently reminding us, and it tends to treat us as we treat it.

I have allowed myself to expound upon the concept of *xenia* only because its practice is essential to the thought of the artist. That art which would enslave the stranger-world is merely propaganda;[2] art worthy of the name must approach the world with love, taking interest in the world not even for the sake of a poem or a picture or a sculpture but merely for the pleasure of it, the joy of being. Art must approach the stranger not with an eye toward enslaving it but with inquisitiveness and delight in it for what it is.

Now, the writer's task, as Joseph Conrad once wrote, is "by the power of the written word to make you hear, to make you feel—it is, before all, to make you see." This is as true of the poet's task as of the novelist's. The task is to make the reader see. But what does Conrad mean by "see"? He means something more by "seeing" than merely allowing images of visible objects to enter into our retinas, for the writer does not work with visible objects like a painter, but with words. Conrad means that the writer must use words that present visible objects to the reader's imagination, and that, simultaneously, present those visible objects in such a way as to reveal both the objects themselves and something about the individual who sees them, to reveal the invisible through the visible.

We are accustomed to a kind of seeing blindness, to seeing objects without seeing them. Anyone who has endured a regular commute over a long period of time knows that, after a while, you may arrive at your destination with no distinct memory of anything you saw along the way. Did you have your eyes closed the whole time? Possibly. (The drivers on I-95 around D.C. seem not to be very aware of their surroundings.) But, more likely, we simply allow the woods along the shoulders and the wildflowers of highway medians and the great sky and the other cars to wash over us like a wave; we observe these objects, but we observe them passively. We do not actively contemplate what we see any more than we actively contemplate the objects in our homes on a daily basis. Who contemplates a couch each time he sits down? Who contemplates that picture on the wall every time she sees it?

In our time, the active contemplation of visible phenomena is a difficult task, one perhaps more difficult than in times past. The primary difficulty is very old: habit and familiarity blunt our senses, make us take for granted the strange things we gather around us. The object that engaged us so deeply in a store window—that made us dream of its future uses, and of who we might be and of how we might be perceived if we possessed the object—becomes, after we have possesssed it for some time, yet another overlooked thing in our cluttered rooms. The glitter of possibility dims, and what was once a prize now gathers dust, or hangs in the back of the closet.

Another, and a newer, impediment to seeing actively is the sensory overload of daily life. We see so much so quickly that very little makes an impression. Our televisions and our computers and our ubiquitous cell-phones are forever presenting images to our sight. The people around us in our overcrowded cities, the construction crews and party-goers and pedestrians and cars and so forth are forever making noise. We are distracted by a thousand distractions, and we distract ourselves from these distractions with further distractions, skimming along on the surface of our lives like leaves on the surface of a stream. We lack the time, and perhaps even the will, to slow down and to contemplate things, to let an image or a sound or a phrase cast its spell over us and possess us. It is ordinary to want to possess things, but extraordinary to want to *be possessed* by things; it is ordinary to want to talk, but extraordinary to want to listen. Like the faces of people in a crowd, the images and sounds and smells of our days pass by us undistinguished, unidentified, uncontemplated, and unknown.

For those who would be poets, these difficulties present two problems. First, the poet himself must find a way to machete a trail through the thick growths of noise, must find a passage through the blur of everyday experience, through the haze of habit and familiarity, in order to experience the world afresh. Secondly, after the poet has performed the first task, he must contrive a way to translate what he has seen into words that have, themselves, the ability to cut through the noise and blur and haze of the reader's life, for the poet must compete for an audience's attention not only with television, movies, the internet, iPhones, video games, radios, and the like, but also with the culture's general tendency toward noise and blur and haze.

The two motions—the motion away from the noise and

the blur of everyday life toward individual vision, and the motion of the return to everyday life and an audience—are what I would call the necessary *turns* in the development of the poet. To think like a poet, both turns are necessary, as one cannot write poetry of any merit without seeing, in the sense Conrad means, and one cannot write poetry that can be read and understood if one cannot communicate what one has seen to others. Both turns are essential to the poet, and both are difficult, often-solitary endeavors that may take years, may, indeed, take a lifetime, for active engagement with the world and writing well require more than merely flipping a "Poetry" switch and leaving that switch in the "ON" position; active engagement with the world and writing well require strenuous effort day after day, require us, in the words of Samuel Beckett, to "Fail again. Fail better." Just as the Christian knows he will sin, but continues to strive toward the impossible perfection of living like Christ, so the poet knows he will have hours and days when he fails his calling, but he continues to strive toward living a life of active engagement and toward the impossible perfection of communicating his vision exactly in language.

The first turn, the turn toward seeing for ourselves, is one that I will call, for lack of a better name, the "Romantic turn." I use the term "Romantic" not with the intention of summoning up pre-existing definitions or conceptions of Romanticism; rather, I use the term in a personal, and perhaps eccentric, way, *faute de mieux*, in order to describe a particular psychic function. This Romantic turn is one we are often too frightened to make because we fear that it will alienate us, make us strange, isolate us from our fellows. The comfort of fitting in, of assuming what others assume, is not to be underestimated; as Flannery O'Connor once wrote, "We all prefer comfort to joy." But the poet cannot be satisfied with comfort, with ease, with getting along and getting by. Rather, the poet is, as Horace once said, a *genus irritabile*, an irritable type, a discontented kind of person; indeed, the poet is like the bird in Marianne Moore's great poem, "What Are Years?" Of that bird, Moore writes, "though he is captive, / his mighty singing / says, satisfaction is a lowly / thing, how pure a thing is joy. / This is mortality, / this is eternity." We are all, like Moore's bird, captive; we have busy lives, responsibilities, actions and distractions to deal with, but the first turn of the poet, the Romantic turn, requires us to ward off complacence and comfort and satisfaction in our cages, requires us to seek something more, something outside the cage.

This seeking of something outside the cage cannot be done haphazardly, or half-heartedly, and the commitment it requires discourages many would-be poets from continuing to develop. The great Austrian poet, Rilke, in his famous poem, "The Archaic Torso of Apollo," has the broken statue of the god of poetry tell us, "You must change your life." And that is what all poetry, worthy of the name, tells us again and again: you must change your life. The Romantic turn is the beginning of this change; it is a turn against complacence and habit, against comfort and the easy way, against the blur and the noise that our culture tells us is all there is of life. It must be made continually.

How does one go about making the Romantic turn? The first step, the easiest step, is simply to clear a space in your life, to find regularly a time and place to be alone, in relative silence, and to contemplate the objects you see. In this contemplation, you must try to see objects, whether natural or man-made, anew, to see them with an active vision that not only notes and names the qualities of the object but also engages the imagination. In many ways, this process is akin to that favorite activity of children: watching clouds and saying what the clouds bring to mind. This one is an elephant; that one a giraffe; that one a beluga whale. The Romantic turn requires us to note that the grass in autumn is not just "green," as we would say, if asked; rather, there's a sort of minty greenish-white, and there's a saffron yellow; there are hints of russet orange, and there's a tawny camel-colored tan, and a deeper chestnut-mare brown; there's jade, and rufous ochre, and hazel, and there's even, in places where the saffron grass and the grass that's still a deep jungle green have been for some time trampled down together, a kind of ghost of a blue or damson that hovers just at the edge of the sight. The Romantic turn requires this sort of visual specificity, the distinguishing of particulars, and the engagement of the imagination as well—what does such multi-colored grass remind you of? A patchwork quilt? Joseph's coat of many colors? The tesserae of a mosaic? A kaleidoscope? A dimly lit stained-glass window? The poet learns to trust his responses. Many will be silly, or non-sense, or downright weird, but the poet must trust that some of these associative responses, sometimes, will point toward deeper connections, toward unforeseen likenesses that bring out the nature of the seen object, or the nature of the seer himself, or both.

We are unaccustomed to such seeing, and its unfamiliarity makes it more difficult, especially at the beginning. We are so accustomed to worrying about being right or wrong, to worrying about fitting in, to worrying about ideas and meanings, that we face profound difficulty whenever we try to *see* anything without immediately imposing some idea or structure on it, whenever we try to approach what we see with xenia, not turning it to some immediate use. But the poet must simply see, before considering ideas or meanings or interpretations, must see with an eye not even toward making a poem, but with the dual ambitions of seeing things for what they are, and of "giving each thing," as Boris Pasternak once said, "its right name." To see things as they are; to give things their right name: these are tasks that require more than the mere gathering of information from Google or from from textbooks. T.S. Eliot once asked, "Where is the wisdom we have lost in knowledge? Where is the knowledge we have lost in information?" Our days are filled with the search for information, and, at best, with the search for knowledge, but wisdom—that knowledge that is personal and earned from careful observation and careful thought and long engagement with the thinkers of the past—is not something we make much time for. The Romantic turn is the beginning of the search for wisdom, for a personal knowledge of the world, a first-hand knowledge of the world, and of ourselves.

Furthermore, to pursue this wisdom, to make the Romantic turn, is counter-cultural in that to make this turn is to acknowledge that we, as individuals, have value, that we are not meant to be all alike, that our differences are, in fact, a great portion of what makes us valuable, for we are, each of us, unique, in that word's true sense, each one of a kind. While science values the individual specimen only to the extent it represents the norms of the genus or species, and while our culture increasingly seeks conformity, the poetic sensibility, like the religious sensibility, sees the value of the individual. No other person will ever live your life, or know what you know exactly in the way you know it. Ephesians 2:10 says, "For we are his handiwork, created in Christ Jesus for the good works that God has prepared in advance, that we should live in them." Now, I want to push on a few words from this passage, looking to the Pauline Greek. The passage opens αὐτοῦ γάρ ἐσμεν ποίημα: *autou* or "His"; *gar* or "for"; *esmen* or "we are"; *poiema*. For we are His *poiema*. *Poiema* is, fairly obviously, the same Greek word from which we get the word, "poem," and one way to read this phrase is that *we are God's poem.*

Such a notion proves illustrative. In poems, each word must have its individual function, and it must work in harmony with all the other words. The words may all be different and mean different things, but all those meanings work together in harmony to make the meaning of the poem. Indeed, this passage in Ephesians suggests that, if we follow the paths God has planned for us individually, we will find communal harmony, but before we can achieve this communal harmony, we must discern and follow our own individual paths (the Greek word translated "we should live" is actually περιπατήσωμεν, *peripatesomen*, or "we should *walk*," as in "peripatetic"). We may achieve a superficial harmony by merely going along with the crowd, but the deeper harmony, the true harmony, comes not from denying our individuality and our differences but from discerning and following the individual paths God intends for us, the way that, in a poem, each word has its own individual meaning that harmonizes with the individual meanings of all the other words to create a greater meaning.

Now this consideration of harmony with others brings us to the second turn, or what I will call the "Classical turn." If the Romantic turn is the turn toward our own individuality, the Classical turn is a return toward our common humanity, and provides the necessary complement to the Romantic turn if we are to think like poets. Sadly, all too often the Classical turn thwarts would-be poets because it seems "unpoetic." We have no problem imagining a poet as a solitary person, wandering through nature and dreaming private dreams. In fact, this image of the poet is the Romantic stereotype. But the actual poet must do more than wander and dream; he must write poems, and he must write poems using words that other people recognize, for language is shared. How, then, can one fit one's personal wisdom, the hard-earned vision of the Romantic turn, into a common language, a language that is constantly being degraded and made clumsy by a reliance on inaccuracies and clichés, and one that is, furthermore, ever-evolving?

Many a would-be poet confronts this question and despairs. It is so difficult to say just what we mean, to say just what we feel, just what we see. The difficulty of doing so is, in fact, why clichés and inaccurate language are so dominant; we shirk the difficult task of exactitude and allow our individual experiences, so nuanced and particular, to be conformed to types, like smashing a square block into a round hole. We say the soccer match was an "emotional roller-coaster," and the recent election was an "emotional roller-coaster," and the death of a friend was "an emotional roller-coaster," blurring the distinctions between our experiences, allowing the particulars to be rounded off. But if we have exerted the time and effort to see with an individual vision, we cannot be satisfied with such rounding off, such blurring. We must find a way to articulate the particular, to make the stranger we have welcomed welcome among our fellows.

This is the part of being a poet they never show in the movies. This is where the poet becomes a craftsman, a "maker," which is the original sense of the word "poet": a *maker*. The Classical turn requires the poet to *make* a poem, to make an aesthetic object, as a painter makes a painting, and a carpenter makes a cabinet, and a stonemason makes a wall. The Romantic turn toward seeing is not enough; the poet must now think about how to make a poem capable of containing and communicating his vision. And the necessity of making, the Classical turn, requires a different kind of work, a kind of unglamorous work that, from the outside, seems arduous and tedious, but for the poet is actually a work of great joy.

The Classical turn requires, first, a mastery of technique. One must learn about meter, not because a teacher says so, but because meter allows poets to create meaning. Meter is not merely an abacus for counting syllables out, though far too many teachers present it as such to rightfully bewildered students; no, meter is a method for capturing in words, which are sounds, the particulars of the poet's vision. The most fanatical metricists are not stodgy old teachers but *poets*, who rejoice in discovering ways in which the sounds of words can work in harmony with their vision. Writing poems without regular meter is, Robert Frost said, like "playing tennis without a net"; it can be done, certainly, but it is much more difficult, because the sounds of a poem, the cadences of a poem, must mean. Indeed, the sounds of a poem *are* meaningful, whether we like it or no, for language is fundamentally comprised of meaningful sounds; to learn meter, then, is merely to learn how to control the meaning of sounds. "There is no escape from meter," as T.S. Eliot once said, "there is only mastery." And to return to Mr. Frost's figure of the tennis net, we might add that it is easier to generate and to control the meanings of our sounds within a restricted context, such as a poem with a regular meter, than in an unrestricted context, such as a poem without a regular meter, for the same reason that it is easier to know whether or not a backhand has gone over the net when there is a visible net present. All English speech and writing inherently possesses a meter; the only question is whether or not the writer controls the meter and makes a meangingful pattern of it. The would-be poet who neglects meter has no more right to the name of "poet" than the artist who can't draw has to the name of "artist," or than the musician who can't keep time has to the name "musician." Of course, I do not intend to suggest that all poems must have regular meters, only to suggest that the meter, whether regular or irregular, must possess a meaingful pattern.

But meter is only one element of poetry. In fact, every element of a poem must be meaningful if we are to capture the strangeness of the individual vision within common words, if we are to articulate the particular, for the words must be forced to do more than they ordinarily do; they must be freighted with more weight than they ordinarily carry.

As the great French poet, Paul Verlaine, wrote in his famous "Art Poétique": "nothing but nuance! / Oh! nuance alone marries / dream to dream." Why is nuance so important? Why must a poem's words do so much more work than ordinary language? The question is a complex one, but here's a brief answer. Language moves in a straight line, a horizontal line, through time, with a sequential order, one syllable following another; however, our experiences are not perfectly linear, nor perfectly sequential. We may remember a multitude of past experiences in a simultaneous burst while contemplating an object in the present. In fact, we do so all the time. All the time, we live in two worlds, a world outside ourselves and a world inside ourselves, and to represent this complexity of experience accurately and fully, language must have recourse to more than its usual means. It must rely on nuance, and meter, like the other figures and tropes we study in literature classes, constitutes a form of nuance, a way of creating a meaning that we might call "vertical," which supplements the linear, horizontal meaning to create a more full-bodied meaning, one capable of containing the complexities of our real experiences, which so often move in more than one direction at a time.

So you must master meter, not just learning the terms and so on, but learning to apply meter meaningfully at will and, eventually, unconsciously. And you must master tone, the use of diction, the use of syntax, the use of linebreaks and the use of images. You must learn and master all those elements of poems and figures of speech that you've probably studied in classes, and that are present in most trustworthy textbooks on poetry, not with an eye toward getting an "A," or toward pleasing a teacher or a parent, but with an eye toward learning how you may allow others entrance into your private vision, how you may use language with xenia, not merely to *communicate* but to create *community*, shared understanding, shared feeling, shared thought.

In order to master these techniques, the poet finds that he must read deeply and broadly in other poets, and in writers of prose, to learn how these same fundamental tools—sound, image, tone, etc.— have been put to different uses. Many young poets believe that reading lots of poetry will impinge on their creativity; this is simply not the case.

Rather, learning the many ways in which language can make communal the private vision facilitates the process of expressing your vision, in the same way that having seen other cabinets facilitates the process of building a cabinet of your own, and that having learned how to use a saw, a hammer, nails, and so forth, facilitates building your cabinet. Furthermore, having seen other cabinets will not mean the cabinet you make is any less your own; rather, having seen a wide variety of other cabinets will allow you greater freedom in determining how you'd like to make your own cabinet, what features you would like to take from this or that cabinet that already exists in order to make a new cabinet that is precisely what you want your cabinet to be.

Now, thus far I have discussed the Romantic and the Classical turns as if they were two separate things. To some extent, they are. The general spiritual motion of youth is toward individuation—the Romantic turn—and age generally brings with it the motion toward solidarity—the Classical turn. But the developed poet's thought performs both turns simultaneously; the developed poet's thought is a synthesis of these turns, a circle whose circumference is the completion of the two semi-circles described by the two turns, a globe that unites the two hemispheres. That is, the poet seeks in his poem to unify the particular and the general, the personal and the universal, the temporal and the eternal. In this sense, to think like a poet is always to move between two worlds, between two realms, to be both guest and host at once.

The ancients believed that man first received language from the god they called Hermes, or Mercury, who was the messenger god. The Greeks also gave Hermes the epithet, *ho psychopompos*, which means "the guide of souls," because Hermes was the god who ushered the souls of the dead down to Hades. I introduce the figure of Hermes because he has long served as a figure for the poet, and, given what we've said, you may see why. As Hermes could move between the eternal realm of the gods and the temporal realm of men, and also between the living and the dead, serving as a link between what would otherwise be separate realities, so the poet must move between realms, between his personal vision and the communal language, between the past and the present, the interior world and the exterior world, the strange and the familiar. For these reasons, it may be useful to think of the poet as psychopomp, a mover between realms, like Hermes.

And, indeed, the mouthpieces for poets have often enough, throughout Western literature, been Hermetic figures, or psychopomps. When Hermes himself appears in book XXIV of the *Iliad* to reconcile the conquered Priam and the conqueror Achilles, and to reconcile the living Achilles to the dead Hector, we catch a glimpse of what Homer the poet was after with his poem. Similarly, when Odysseus, after descending into Hades in book XI of the *Odyssey*, returns to Ithaka, we may see connections between Odysseus, Homer himself, and the psychopomp, Hermes, who appears in a parallel scene in book XXIV, for each moves between worlds to bring about a kind of order. Orestes, in Aeschylus' *Oresteia*, moves between the chthonic world of the past and the new world of reason to bring about a new order, the Athenian Areopagus; similarly, Portia in Shakespeare's *Merchant of Venice* moves between the magical realm of Belmont and the mercantile world of Venice to restore order through Christian mercy, and so forth and so on. (It's worth noting that "merchant" and "mercy," the two crucial and apparently oppositional terms in Shakespeare's play, both have etymological ties to "Mercury," Hermes' Roman name). One could go on listing famous works that include Hermetic figures, or psychopomps, and, in doing so, one would name almost every great work in the Western tradition—from the *Iliad* to the *Divine Comedy* to *The Waste Land*—but the point is that these figures are always out to bring order and harmony to the world, to reconcile differences, to teach xenia, and thereby to create unity out of disunity, and the reason poets are forever turning to such figures is that to create such a unity is the goal of poetry.

We generally live in a world of fragments: we go to school, and go to work, and go to parties, and go to church, but we rarely think of how what we learned in school applies to what we see at a party, and rarely see how what we experience at church relates to what we're studying in architecture or economics, or to the latest problem at our jobs. To think like a poet is to seek to unite the fragments, to seek a full and unified vision of life that includes the individuality and uniqueness of each experience and of each individual and *also* allows for the commonality shared by individuals and experiences, the patterns that bind us together, for the poet is like the psychopomp attempting to build a bridge between worlds, and poetry *is* and *has been*, from its beginnings, not about being cool or mysterious or sad or "deep," but about the health of the human spirit, which cannot be healthy without xenia, cannot be healthy when it denies the inner life, or the outer life, cannot be healthy when it denies the past, or the present, or the future, when it denies life, or death, the visible, or the invisible. The healthy soul, like the gracious host, must welcome every stranger.

Indeed, as Keats wrote in an 1817 letter to Benjamin Bailey: "Men of Genius are great as certain ethereal chemicals operating on the Mass of neutral intellect—but they have not any individuality, any determined character—I would call the top and head of those who have a proper self Men of Power." The poet, lacking a "proper self," sees himself as a stranger. He is not, like a Man of Power, out to assert his will, but his task lies in abandoning his own will and his own desires in order to merge imaginatively with other people, even with inanimate objects, and with ideas. This ability, which Keats elsewhere called "negative capability" is tantamount to Humility, to the virtue of selflessness, which is, *mutatis mutandis*, the ancient quality of *xenia*.

And this brings us back to our opening remarks. Teachers and students alike often talk about poetry and literature as if they exist only for the sake of their ideas. If such were the case, there would be no point in literature, for its ability to handle ideas falls far short of philosophy's ability to do so. And if we are concerned only with ideas, or even with truth, we had better turn to fields other than literature and poetry, for, in the modern sense of "truth," the truth value of some of the greatest poetry is almost nil beside that of science, psychology, theology, and other disciplines. Happily, literature and poetry do not exist only for their ideas. And this is the answer to the question students are forever asking: "Why doesn't the poet come right out and say what he means?"

The poet *does say* what he means; the reader, however, is often unprepared for meaning of the kind the poet makes, for truth of the poetic kind. The poet's meaning is symbolic, is a unity of body and idea, of the concrete and abstract, the physical and metaphysical, and it is a unity that is indissoluble. To isolate either part is to distort the symbol's meaning by reducing it: the symbol means as we mean, who have both bodies and souls. The symbol represents a full human reality; it has both a physical reality and a metaphysical significance. While the contemporary reader generally wants meaning to exist in abstract ideas alone, separate from the world of the senses and objects, the poet thinks through the senses; that is, thinking is not, for the poet, separate from seeing and hearing and feeling. The realm of abstract ideas is united with the realm of sensory perception in a symbolic vision.

If we understand this, if we understand how the particular act of the Israelites escaping Egypt takes on universal significance while maintaining its literal and historical reality, we are prepared to think like poets. The poet sees universals, or ideas, or meanings—however we want to call them—within particulars, within actions and objects, not separate from them. Now some poets tend to focus more on particulars, and others more on universals, but any poet worth the name makes both the Romantic turn and the Classical turn, seeing the particular afresh, and representing that vision in such a way as to make it available to others.

Art is symbolic. Art is incarnation. It is giving body to thought, or binding thought and body. To write poetry, then, we must learn to greet the stranger-world with xenia, to see it for what it is, and then we must learn to name what we see. The first is the Romantic turn, the second is what I have called the Classical. But, as I've said, the two turns are interconnected: we often learn to name by seeing, and learn to see by naming. Think, for instance, of walking through the woods. If you don't know the names of the trees, you see yourself surrounded by a green mass of trees. But if you learn the names of the particular trees, suddenly you see the trees themselves more clearly, more distinctly: the naming helps you see. Similarly, seeing the shape of a maple leaf, or the bark of a birch, helps you to name the tree.

The poet is always seeing and naming, always guest and host, always moving back and forth at once, a psychopomp, a Hermes, seeing and responding, always active, always looking for new unities, new correspondences, new wholes, each new discovery reorganizing and redefining those that came before.[3] To think like a poet is never to be bored again. To think like a poet is, ultimately, to practice xenia to the stranger-world, to seek the unity and harmony of body and soul, of object and subject, seen and seer, to seek those moments when the individual and fragmented takes its place in a greater pattern. To think like a poet is to make the invisible motions of the spirit visible, to make the silent revolutions of the soul clap hands and sing, as we clap hands and sing at wedding receptions, for a poem is a wedding of the worlds.

NOTES

1. In our time, a great deal of "art" could more accurately be called "anti-art," or, if we are more blunt, "bad art." The preponderance of anti-art does not change what "art" itself is any more than the preponderance of children's finger-paintings should make us change our understanding of Michelangelo's paintings, or any more than the preponderance of sin changes what grace is.

2. We too often think of propaganda as an absolute substance, when it is actually more of a process. That is, effective propaganda possesses many of the attributes of art, which is why it is so effective; what separates propaganda from genuine art is that the propagandist forces his material to comply with his will, rather than allowing his materials to exist independent of his will. In this, the propagandist is similar to a god who does not allow men free will, or to the sentimentalist.

3. It is no coincidence that this circular relationship, in which we understand the whole from the parts and the parts from the whole, is called the 'Hermeneutic Circle,' for Hermes, who moves back and forth between worlds, has given it its name.

Acknowledgments

I offer my sincere thanks to Joshua Hren, Mary Finnegan, and Wiseblood Books for their xenia. Thanks also to Bernardo Aparacio García, the former Editor of *Dappled Things*, in which "How to Think Like a Poet" was first published, and to James Matthew Wilson, who awarded this piece the Jacques Maritain Prize.

Special thanks are due to Dr. Kevin Rulo, who first suggested that I write the piece as a lecture at The Catholic University of America, and also to Dana Gioia, Virgil Nemoianu, Taryn Okuma, Joan Romano Shifflett, and Ernest Suarez, all of whom have supported this project.

Additional thanks are due to: Austin Allen, Mike Aquilina, Brian Brodeur, Chris Childers, George David Clark, the late Msgr. John Cuddy, Armen Davoudian, Caitlin Doyle, John Glass, Rachel Hadas, Ernest Hilbert, Raphael Krut-Landau, Brad Leithauser, Robert Pinsky, Mary Jo Salter, Dave Smith, Rosanna Warren, and David Yezzi.

Most of all, I am grateful to my mother, Dr. Martha Wilson, and to Matthew Buckley Smith for their indefatigable support.

About Ryan Wilson

Ryan Wilson was born in Griffin, GA, and raised in nearby Macon. He is the author of *The Stranger World* (Measure, 2017), winner of the Donald Justice Poetry Prize, of *Proteus Bound: Selected Translations, 2008-2020* (Franciscan UP, 2021), and of *In Ghostlight: Poems* (2024), published by LSU in their Southern Messenger Poets Series. His work appears widely in periodicals such as *32 Poems*, *First Things*, *Five Points*, *The Hopkins Review*, *Image*, *The New Criterion*, *The Sewanee Review*, and *The Yale Review*, and has been anthologized in *Best American Poetry*, *Christian Poetry in America Since 1940*, *Poetry Daily*, *Verse Daily*, and elsewhere. For many years the Editor-in-Chief of *Literary Matters*, he is co-editor (with April Lindner) of *Contemporary Catholic Poetry: An Anthology* (Paraclete, 2024), a finalist for the Foreword Book Prize. He teaches in the M.F.A. program at The University of St. Thomas-Houston, and he lives in small-town Texas.

WISEBLOOD ESSAYS IN CONTEMPORARY CULTURE

Wiseblood Essays in Contemporary Culture offer in-depth interpretations of literature and art at large from a distinctly Catholic vantage point, while also championing and criticizing notable Catholic contributions to culture.

SELECTED TITLES

The Wayward Thomist:
A Critical Introduction to John Martin Finlay
James Matthew Wilson

A Theology of Fiction
Cassandra Nelson

Jane Austen's Darkness
Julia Yost

The Catholic Writer Today
Dana Gioia

"Everything Came to Me at Once":
The Intellectual Vision of René Girard
Cynthia L. Haven

Duty, the Soul of Beauty: Henry James on the Beautiful Life
R. R. Reno

The Tragedy of the Republic
Pierre Manent

Death Comes for the Cathedrals
Marcel Proust

Poetry and Mysticism
Raïssa Maritain

T. S. Eliot: Culture and Anarchy
James Matthew Wilson

www.ingramcontent.com/pod-product-compliance
Lightning Source LLC
Chambersburg PA
CBHW052128070526
44586CB00016B/2128